LEARN ABOUT JAPAN

For Kids

From the Learn About the World Series

ISBN 978-1-7390565-6-8

LEARN ABOUT JAPAN

For Kids

This Book Belongs to:

____

Learn About Japan Contents

Learn About Japan Contents

Where is Japan?

Japan is a fascinating country in East Asia. It lies east of Russia and west of the United States, surrounded by the Pacific Ocean. If you're flying from North America, you may have to zoom around the whole planet to get to Japan. But here's a cool fact: because our Earth is a big, round sphere, the trip is shorter than you'd guess. It's like taking a shortcut on a globe!

The Main Islands of Japan

Japan has 6,852 islands. People live on 430 of those, leaving 6,422 islands uninhabited.

The four main islands of Japan are Hokkaido, Honshu, Shikoku and Kyushu. Some people count Okinawa as a main island, making it five.

The Language

The main language spoken in Japan is called Japanese.

The Japanese language uses three unique scripts—kind of like sets of letters—called Hiragana, Katakana, and Kanji. Hiragana has 46 characters and is usually the first script learned by Japanese children.

On the next page, we'll use English letters, like the ones you're reading now, to show you how to say some Japanese words. We'll also teach you how to pronounce these words so you can practice saying them.

Because if we showed you this is how to say "thank you" in Japanese, you might scratch your head in wonder!

ありがとう

Polite Words/Phrases

Whenever you travel to a place with another language, it's always polite to try and learn a few phrases. Let's learn some basic Japanese phrases:

- Hello
- Konnichiwa (koh-nee-chee-wah)

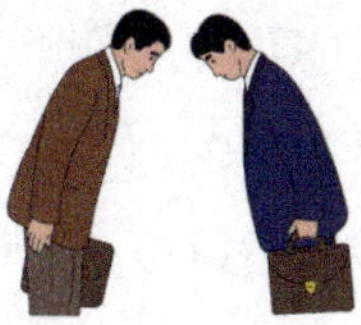

- Goodbye
- Sayōnara (sah-yoh-nah-rah)

- Please
- Onegaishimasu (oh-neh-gah-ee-shee-mahs)

- Thank you
- Arigatō (ah-ree-gah-toh)

- Excuse me / I'm sorry / (or used to get someone's attention, like a waiter)
- Sumimasen (soo-mee-mah-sen)

Money in Japan

In Japan, the money they use is called the Japanese Yen, and you'll see it written like this: ¥.

Their money is super tough because it's made from a mix of special paper and pulp. To make sure no one tries to make fake money, they have secret tricks like watermarks and shiny holograms that change when you look at them from different angles.

When it comes to paper money, there are 1,000, 2,000, 5,000, and 10,000 yen bills.

¥500 coin

The coins are 1, 5, 10, 50, 100, and 500 yen coins.

The ¥500 coin is really high-tech! It's made from two types of metal, has writing on the side, and a certain pattern that is hard to copy.

Fun Fact: The ¥1 coin is made of aluminum and is so light you can barely feel it in your hand.

The Japanese Flag

The Japanese flag is called the Hinomaru (hee-noh-mah-roo). It has a big red circle in the middle that looks like the sun. That's because Japan is often called 'the land of the rising sun.'

The red circle, or sun, has been on Japan's flag for a very long time, but it was officially made the national flag in 1999.

There's another flag called the Rising Sun Flag, or Kyokujitsu-ki, which means 'sunrise flag'. It has red rays coming out from the sun. It was used a long time ago by the military, but nowadays, it's mainly seen at special celebrations.

The Weather in Japan

Japan is shaped like a long, stretched-out ribbon, reaching from the cold north to the warm south. This means the weather in Japan can be very different depending on where you are, just like how the weather can change from one place to another in your own country.

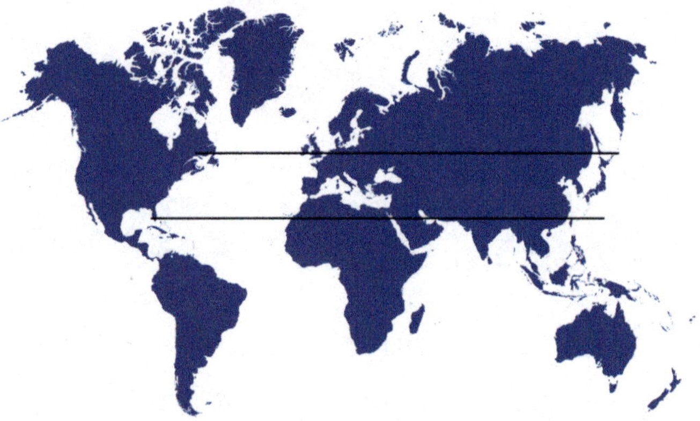

Let's pretend we have a piece of string stretching from the top of Japan to the bottom, including Okinawa, which is way down in the south. If we took this string and laid it across the globe, it would be like comparing the weather in southern England to Egypt or from the cool Maritime Canada to the warm beaches of southern Florida.

Now, let's focus on Japan's five main areas. If we look at the temperatures in January and then in July, there's a big change! Just like sometimes you wear a coat and other times shorts, people in Japan also have to change what they wear often because of the weather changes.

	Hokkaido	Honshu	Shikoku	Kyushu	Okinawa
JANUARY	-3°c 26.6°f	4°c 39.2°f	5°c 41°f	5°c 41°f	19°c 66.2°f
JULY	21°c 69.8°f	27°c 80.6°f	27°c 80.6°f	27°c 80.6°f	29°c 84.2°f

Climates

Hokkaido

Summers are mild, with less rain and humidity than the rest of Japan. Winters can have heavy snowfalls.

Honshu

Summers are hot and humid, and winters are cold, especially in the north of the region. There is more snow on the West Coast than on the East Coast.

Shikoku and Kyushu

Summers are hot and humid. There is a lot of rain in the summer, especially during the monsoon season (June - July). Winters are dry with not a lot of snow.

Okinawa

Tropical rainforest climate. Warm to hot all year round. The rainy season starts in May, with typhoons more common in July and August.

The Population of Japan

As of 2024, Japan's population was about 122.6 million, but it has been decreasing, which worries the government. To help, they've started new programs to make it easier for young couples to afford homes and care for their kids, hoping families will feel supported to have more children.

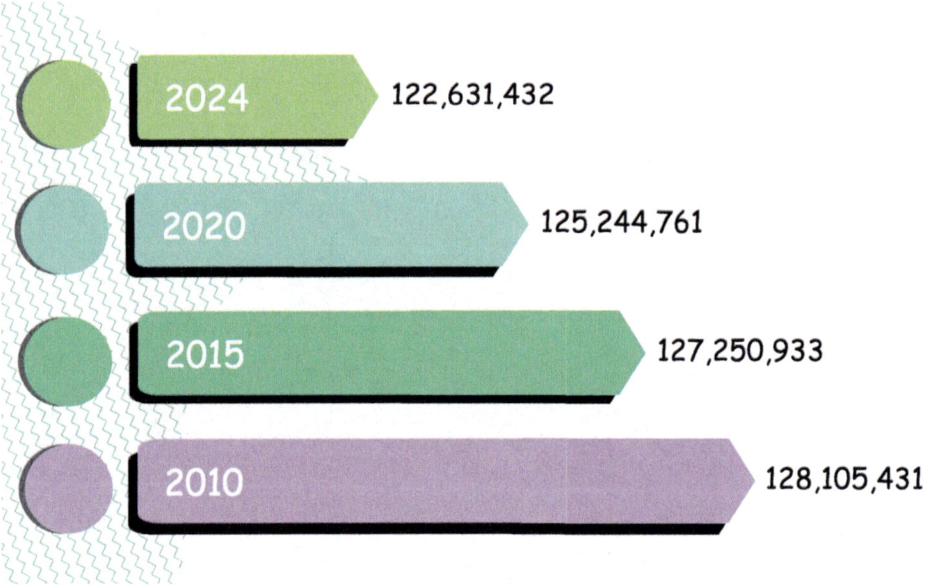

The median (average) age in Japan is 49.1. This means half the population is younger than 49.1, and half is older.

median age is 49.1 years old

Population Density

Population density is how many people are squished into a space as big as a soccer field, which is about one square kilometre (km^2). To figure it out, you take the number of people in a country and see how they fit into the total space of the land. This number tells us if a country feels like a cozy blanket fort or a wide-open park. The higher the number, the less wiggle room everyone has.

Country Population Density

United States	36
United Kingdom	279
Bangladesh	1,265
Denmark	137
Australia	3
Jamaica	273
Germany	233
Italy	200
France	122
Japan	347
Mexico	66
Singapore	8,358
Canada	4

In Japan, 347 people share every square kilometre. But that's just an average for the whole country. If you zoom into Tokyo, the big city has 6,158 people in the same space! Imagine that many people are at a concert or a sports game, all in one square kilometre.

Now think about where you live. How crowded do you think it is?

Where Everyone Lives

The cities with the largest population are:

1. Tokyo about 9 million
2. Osaka 2.7 million
3. Nagoya 2.3 million

Each blue dot represents a city with more than 300,000 people.

Locations are approximate

Fun Fact: About 30% of Japan's population lives in the greater Tokyo area.

Japanese Homes

In every corner of a Japanese home, you can spot something really special. Let's peek at two things you might find:

Sliding Doors (shoji)

These aren't your regular swing-open-and-close doors. Instead, these doors glide smoothly to the side. Made of a wood frame filled in with paper that's as strong as it is delicate, these doors do the job of walls but with a twist. They slide open to make more space or shut tight for some quiet time alone. Plus, they let the breeze in when you open them. Want less light? No problem! Slide the door and it's like pulling down a shade.

Floor Mats (tatami)

Now, look down at the floors. You'll find tatami mats, about 6' x 3' each. They're woven from special grass or straw that smells fresh, like a day out in the fields. These mats aren't just nice to look at; they're cozy under your feet, keeping the chill away and making the room snug. They're good for your health, too, because they keep out the dampness.

Japanese Homes

Most Japanese homes have a covered indoor/outdoor porch called an **engawa**. This space is important because it allows people to enjoy nature while still being part of the inside of the home.

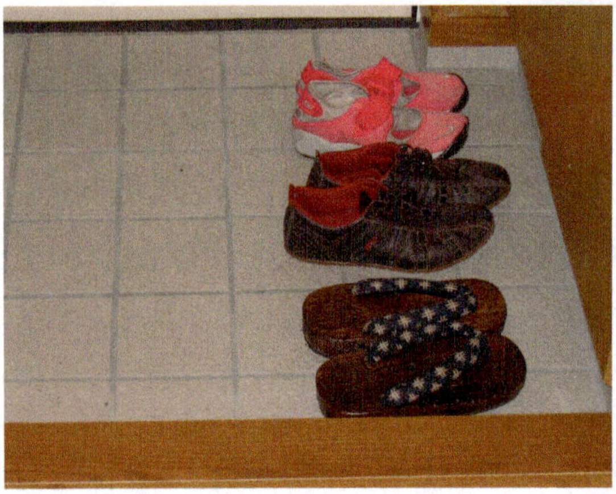

In Japan, you should never wear shoes inside the home. So every entryway has a **genkan**. This is a space to leave your shoes.

Many Japanese homes have a sacred shrine, often to remember and honor family members who have passed away. It's a special spot for reflection and to feel close to loved ones.

Japanese Bathrooms

In Japanese family homes, it's normal to shower and clean yourself thoroughly before getting into the bathtub. This is because the whole family uses the same bath water. Some bathrooms have a control panel on the wall to warm the bath water for the next person. In Japan, taking a bath is more like relaxing in a hot tub.

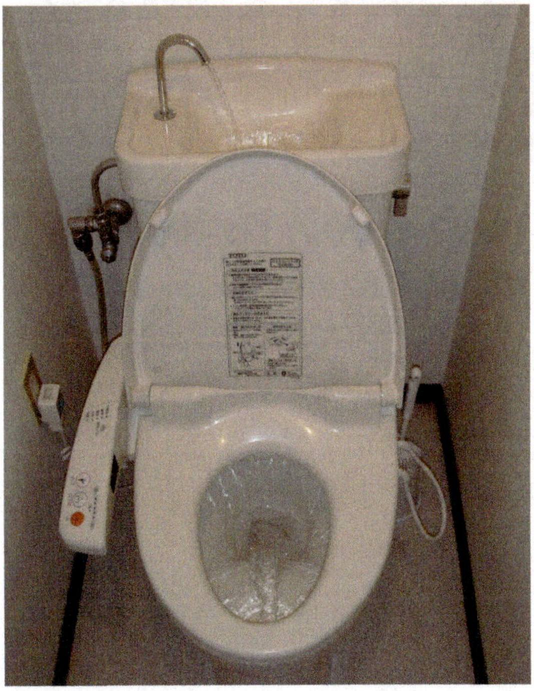

Japanese toilets are super cool! They usually have a bidet, which is a sprayer to clean your bottom, controls to adjust the water temperature, and even a feature to warm up the seat! Also, on some toilets, when you flush, clean water flows out from a tap behind the toilet so you can wash your hands. Then, this water is used to fill up the toilet tank again.

A Brief History of Japan

710 - 794 Japan's capital was called Nara (check out page 30 for more). An emperor named Emperor Shōmu was in charge, and he had a huge and famous Buddhist temple called Tōdai-ji built. After a while, the capital moved to Kyoto.

1010 - The very first novel in the world was written by a mysterious Japanese lady known by her pen name Murasaki Shikibu. We don't know her real name, but her book, "The Tale of Genji," was about Prince Genji and his exciting life, filled with lots of love stories and secrets from the olden days of Japan.

1192 - 1868 Japan was ruled by powerful leaders called shoguns. Even though there was an Emperor, the shoguns were the ones really in charge. They had brave warriors known as samurai to guard them and carry out their commands. These samurai were super-skilled fighters who followed a strict code of honour and bravery.

1397 - The Temple of the Golden Pavilion was built in Kyoto. It's super shiny because its top two floors are covered in gold!

1639 - 1853 Japan had a rule called 'Sakoku' which means they decided to keep the country all to themselves. They did this because lots of Europeans were coming over and trying to change things, like introducing Christianity, and Japan wanted to stay just the way it was.

1853 - American Commodore Matthew Perry sailed to Japan to trade with them, but Japan said "no thanks." However, after some time, they changed their minds. Perry's visit led to Japan opening up and starting to trade not only with America but also with countries like Russia, Britain, France, and Holland.

1868 - The Emperor decided to pack up and go to Edo, a large city in Japan. Once he got there, they changed the name of the city to Tokyo, and it became the brand-new capital of Japan.

1914 - 1918 World War I was happening, and Japan decided to be part of it by declaring war on Germany. When the war was over, Japan was invited to join a special group called the League of Nations. This was a team of countries that worked together, mainly in Switzerland, to solve big problems and try to keep peace all over the world, hoping to avoid more huge wars.

A Brief History of Japan

1940 - 1945 During World War II, Japan was part of a group called the Axis powers, along with Germany and Italy. Japan had already left the League of Nations back in 1933 because of some disagreements. In **1941**, Japan made a surprise attack on Pearl Harbor in Hawaii, which shocked America. Then, in **1945**, America dropped atomic bombs on two Japanese cities, Hiroshima and Nagasaki. These powerful bombs caused so much destruction that Japan decided to stop fighting, and this helped to bring an end to the war.

1951 - 1960 Japan and America became friends again after World War II. In **1951**, they signed a very important agreement called the San Francisco Peace Treaty, which helped Japan become independent again. Then, in **1960**, they made another big agreement called the Treaty of Mutual Cooperation and Security, which meant they promised to help protect each other.

1956 - Japan became a part of a group called the United Nations (UN). They were the 80th country to join. The UN brings countries together to keep peace and support each other.

1960 - 1995 Japan's economy grew a lot because they were amazing at making electronics and cars. They became one of the top countries in the world for this!

1964 - The Olympic Games were a big deal in Tokyo, Japan. Athletes from all around the world came to compete!

1995 - A massive earthquake hit near Kobe, Japan. It was called the Great Hanshin Earthquake Disaster. It was very serious, taking the lives of over 6,400 people and causing damages costing more than $100 billion. Then, in **2011,** another tragic event happened, the Tohoku Earthquake and Tsunami, which was devastating and led to the loss of more than 18,000 lives.

2013 - UNESCO* honoured Mount Fuji by declaring it a cultural world heritage site.

Today - Today, Japan is friends with lots of countries like America, Canada, and the United Kingdom, and is part of a big group called the G20, which includes 20 of the biggest economies in the world. Japan has the fourth-largest economy, which means it's really successful at making and selling things all over the world.

*UNESCO is a group that helps protect important places and traditions around the world.

Japan's Royal Family
The Imperial House of Japan

The Past:

According to old stories, Japan's very first Emperor was a man named Jimmu, who is said to have been in charge around 660 BCE. But there's no real evidence that he existed, so many people think Jimmu is more of a mythical figure, like a character from a fairy tale. Whether he was a myth or not, Japan celebrates February 11 as the day Jimmu was crowned. National Foundation Day is a public holiday (see page 45).

So, this brings up a tricky question: who was the actual first Emperor of Japan? It's hard to separate the fairy tale bits from the actual history when we talk about Japan's royal past. Some history buffs believe that the first real Emperor was Ōjin, who they think ruled from around 270 to 310. But, others argue that Emperor Kinmei was in charge from 539 to 571. And just when you thought it couldn't get more confusing, the official title of "Emperor" didn't even start until Emperor Tenmu, who ruled from 673 to 686. So, it's a bit of a historical puzzle!

The Present:

Since 2019, the Emperor of Japan has been Naruhito, who was born in 1960. He has a daughter named Princess Aiko. But in Japan, the rules say that only men can become Emperor. So, the next person who might become Emperor is Naruhito's younger brother, Crown Prince Akishino. After him, the next in line is Akishino's son, Prince Hisahito, who was born in 2006.

What Does the Emperor do?

The Japanese Emperor and his family, much like the Royal Family in Britain, have roles that are mostly for show and tradition, which means they don't make decisions about the country's laws or politics. But they are still very important in Japan for many reasons.

They go to big events, give out special awards, and have important jobs in ceremonies, like being part of the official process when Japan picks its Prime Minister and Supreme Court Justices, or when the National Diet, which is Japan's government group, starts or finishes its work. The Emperor and his family also meet with important visitors from other countries and go abroad representing Japan, helping to build good relationships with other countries.

School in Japan

The School Year

In Japan, kids spend six years in elementary school, three years in junior high school, and another three in high school. Their school year starts in April and ends in March the next year. They split the year into three parts, with vacations in between. Summer break is the longest, about 40 days, while spring and winter breaks are shorter, around ten days each.

Japanese students have 210 to 220 days of school each year. That's more than in the United States, where students go for about 180 days, and more than in Canada and the UK, which have around 190 days, and even Australia, with 200 days. But it's not all work in Japan; students also enjoy clubs and festivals, choosing from activities like sports, arts, and music.

Exams

In Japan, exams are really important! Kids take big entrance exams to get into high school and university. These exams are a huge deal because they help decide which school you can go to. For university, the test is super tough—some say it's one of the hardest in the world! While junior high schools usually don't have tough entrance exams, getting into a good high school or university can be really challenging.

Uniforms and Style Code

In Japan, most junior high and high school students wear uniforms. But it's not just about the uniform; there are strict rules on how students should look, from their hair to whether they can wear nail polish, and more.

At school, students switch their outdoor shoes for indoor ones, storing them in a special cubby, just like they do at home.

School Duties

Japanese schools are unique because they usually don't have janitors or lunchroom staff. Instead, students help out with tasks like serving lunch and cleaning. They take turns cleaning different parts of the school, including windows, floors, and even toilets. This helps everyone learn how to be responsible and take care of their school environment.

Diverse Landscapes of Japan

Japanese Alps

A series of mountain ranges found on the main island of Honshu.

Coastline

The Japanese coastline covers a total of 29,751 km. About 16% of the coast are beaches, the rest is mostly rocky cliffs.

Forests

Two-thirds of the land area in Japan is made up of forests.

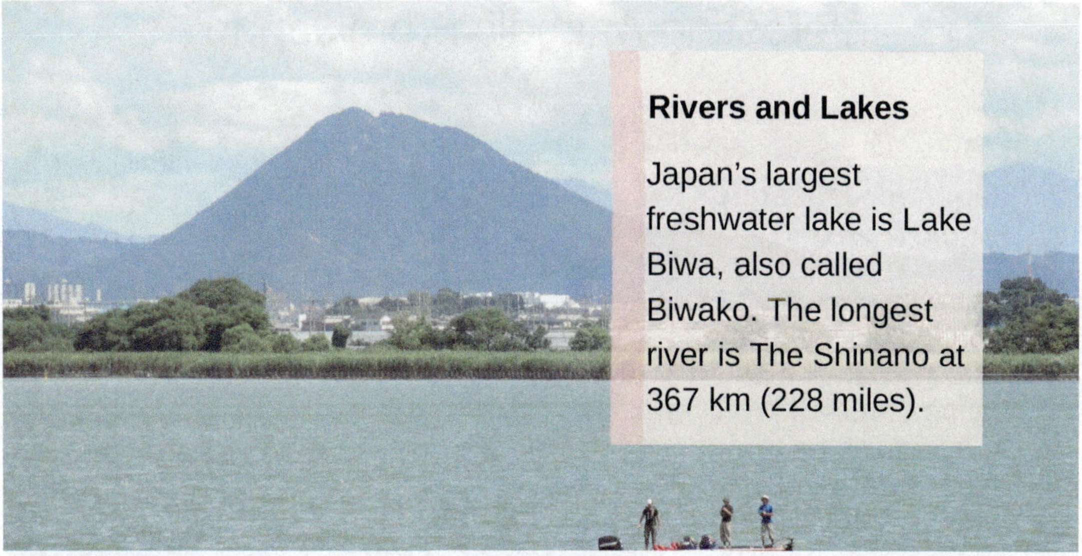

Rivers and Lakes

Japan's largest freshwater lake is Lake Biwa, also called Biwako. The longest river is The Shinano at 367 km (228 miles).

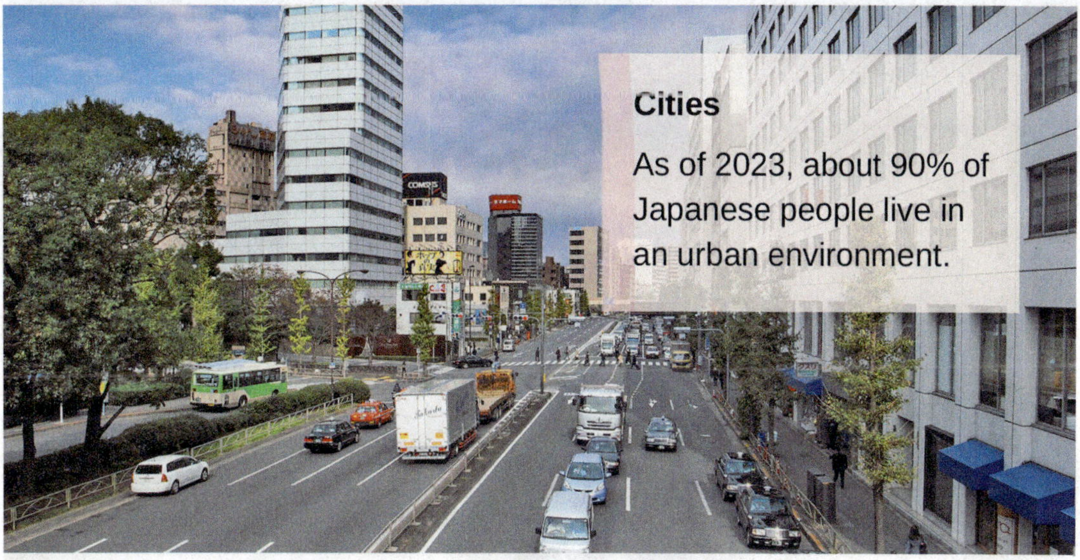

Cities

As of 2023, about 90% of Japanese people live in an urban environment.

Farms

On Japanese farms, the most commonly grown crops include rice, which is the most important, followed by corn, wheat, barley, soybeans, and peanuts.

Interesting Animals From Japan

Japanese Macaque (snow monkey)

The only monkey in the world known to take relaxing baths in hot springs (onsen). You can find them at the Jigokudani Monkey Park near Nagano, Japan (more on page 38).

Japanese Racoon Dog (Tanuki)

Known in Japanese folklore as shape-shifters and are often depicted as playful creatures who wear a straw hat.

Japanese Marten

They love honey so much, they are brave enough to raid beehives!

Creepy Creatures From Japan

Giant Spider Crab

Their leg span can reach 12 feet (3.65 metres)! But don't worry, they live in deep water off the shores of Japan.

Japanese Rhinoceros Beetle

They fight by using their horns to flip their enemies on their back. A popular pet for Japanese Kids!

Asian Giant Hornet (Murder Hornet)

The largest hornet in the world. The queen can reach 2 inches (5cm). They can be found all over Asia, and is native to Japan.

Touring Japan - Map

If you're travelling to Japan, you may be visiting relatives or going as tourists. Or maybe a bit of both. Regardless of where you go in Japan, there are so many wonderful things to see and do.

In this section, we'll look at Japan's top tourist places and give you a bit of what you can expect in each location.

Tokyo

Not only is Tokyo the capital of Japan, but it's also the biggest city there, home to more than 37 million people in its metro area. This makes Tokyo one of the most populated places in the world!

Kids have a blast in Tokyo, especially at **Tokyo Disneyland and Tokyo DisneySea**. These theme parks are different from the American Disney parks because they have many unique and fun twists.

Other cool spots in Tokyo include the **Ghibli Museum,** where animation comes to life; **Kidzania**, where kids can play at being adults; **Ueno Zoo**, full of amazing animals; and **Miraikan**, a museum filled with cool science and technology. If you love Pokemon, you've got to check out the **Pokemon Cafe**, but it's super popular, so you need to book ahead. If it's full, don't worry; you can visit **Pikachu Sweets** right next door.

There is a manmade island in Tokyo Bay that includes a futuristic area called **Odaiba** with many interesting attractions, including a giant Ferris wheel for amazing views of the city.

Kyoto

For over 1,000 years, Kyoto was the heart of Japan and even had more people than Tokyo. "Kyoto" actually means "capital city."

Known as the "city of a thousand shrines," Some must-see spots include the **Kiyomizu-dera Temple** and the **Fushimi-inari-Taisha Shrine**. Plus, there's the **Kamigamo Shrine**, which is 1,300 years old!

Don't miss out on a **rickshaw ride** when you're in Kyoto**.** For some train history**,** explore the **Kyoto Railway Museum.** For a comic book adventure, check out the **Kyoto International Manga Museum**.

Fun Fact: The **Arashiyama Bamboo Grove,** also known as Sagano Bamboo Forest, is a photographer's dream and one of Kyoto's top sights (find out more about this bamboo wonder on page 39).

Nara

Nara was also once the capital of Japan (710 - 794) and is home to the **Seven Great Temples of Nara.**

You can reach Nara from Kyoto or Osaka in under an hour by train, so it's a popular day-trip destination from these major cities.

Nara Park is a must-visit spot where you'll find Tōdai-ji, one of Japan's most famous temples, with a huge 15-meter (49-foot) tall bronze Buddha statue, Daibutsu. Don't miss the Kasuga Taisha Shrine, built in 768, known for its over 3,000 lanterns!

If you get tired of temples, shrines, lanterns and buddhas, you can spend some time with some of the hundreds of deer that roam the park. The deer were once sacred in Japan and are still protected today. The park offers special crackers for sale so you can feed them.

Osaka

Are you someone who loves trying out new foods? Then you've got to visit Osaka! It's known for its delicious street food and friendly vibes, making it a top spot for families.

If you're in Osaka, don't forget to explore the **Osaka Aquarium Kaiyukan** and take a trip to the **Osaka Science Museum***. You'll also find a **Pokemon Cafe** here, just like in Tokyo. Plus, there's **Universal Studios Japan** for some movie magic and thrilling rides.

The city also has beautiful waterfronts and beaches that you can reach by bus. Just a heads-up, though, people usually don't start swimming there until after mid-July.

Fun Fact: Osaka is the birthplace of **takoyaki,** those yummy grilled octopus balls you see on street food stalls. They were first made and perfected right here in Osaka!

*The Osaka Science Museum is temporarily closed for reconstruction as of the writing of this book. It is scheduled to re-open in the summer of 2024.

Sapporo

Sapporo is the biggest city in Hokkaido, the northern island of Japan. It's known for its chilly weather, and in January, it can get really cold, sometimes dropping to around -6ºC (21ºF) or even colder.

One of the most popular spots in Sapporo is the **Kokusai Ski Resort**, known for its amazing powder snow. If you love skiing, you can enjoy it there for half the year, from November all the way to May!

No matter if you go to Sapporo in the snowy winter or the sunny summer, don't forget to visit **Shiroi Koibito Park**. It's a dreamy place with a chocolate factory and a theme park rolled into one.

Fun Fact: Sapporo hosted the Olympic Winter Games in 1972, making it a famous spot for winter sports!

Okinawa

Okinawa is the biggest island in the southern part of the Ryukyu Islands chain. It's pretty warm there most of the year because it has a tropical climate. If your family is dreaming of a beach vacation in Japan, Okinawa is likely the place they're thinking about.

But it's not all about the beach! While you're there, you should also check out the **Churaumi Aquarium.** It's one of the biggest aquariums on the planet and is part of the **Ocean Expo Park.**

People in Okinawa are known for being super healthy and living long. They believe the secrets are healthy living, strong friendships and family ties, and eating good, nutritious food.

Fun Fact: Karate was invented in Okinawa.

Fukuoka

Fukuoka is a seaside city with some nice beaches that are perfect for summer. But there's more to this city than just beach fun! Fukuoka is a mix of history and modern shopping.

Want to see one of the biggest Buddha statues in the world? Visit **Nanzoin Temple** to see the giant reclining Buddha, which is 41 meters (134.5 feet) long and weighs 300 tons!

In Hakata Old Town, you'll find lots of old temples and shrines, like **Jotenji** and **Shofukuji.** And make sure to see **Tochoji Temple**—it has Japan's largest wooden Buddha and an impressive five-story pagoda (temple).

Mount Fuji

Japan's most famous site is Mount Fuji, which is the highest mountain in Japan. As you can tell from its shape, Mount Fuji is a volcano. The last time it erupted was in 1707, more than 300 years ago. But it is still considered an active volcano.

Do people climb Mount Fuji? Absolutely! The trails are open from July to mid-September. Although technically, you could do it in a day; it is strongly recommended that you reserve a hut along the way and spend the night there. The reason is that Mount Fuji is so high up that you could get altitude sickness. Staying overnight allows your body to get used to the height. After dinner and some rest, many people get up at 2:00 or 3:00 a.m., wear a headlamp, and reach the top for a beautiful sunrise.

Climbing Mount Fuji is a popular adventure, and anyone over 8 or 9 years old can do it. Toilets and snack bars along the trails make it possible for anyone in good shape.

Fun Fact: There are vending machines at the top of Mt. Fuji.

Hakone

Hakone is an 80-minute train ride from Tokyo and makes a great day trip to get away from the crowded city.

You can cruise on a pirate ship across **Lake Ashi** and get amazing views of Mount Fuji. The red torii (gate) pictured above is called the **Torii of Peace** and marks the entrance to the **Hakone Shrine.**

Another popular spot is the **Hakone Open-Air Museum**, which has indoor and outdoor displays, including more than 300 works by Picasso. The park has one of the world's largest collections by sculptor Henry Moore. To top off your visit, relax in a foot bath at the museum, set in a long trough with hot spring water, possibly enhanced with citrus slices for an extra refreshing experience. How relaxing!

Japanese Macaque soaking in an onsen

Jigokudani Monkey Park

Japan is famous for its hot-spring-loving monkeys, especially at Jigokudani Monkey Park, the best place to see this unique behavior. The park is about 254 km (157.8 miles) from Tokyo, close to **Nagano**, which hosted the 1998 Winter Olympics and is around 35 km (21.7 miles) from the park.

Getting to the onsen (hot spring) isn't easy, especially in the winter. Once you are at the park entrance by car or bus, you have to walk another 1.6 km (1 mile) through the forest. The path is slippery in the winter, but you can rent grips to put over your boots.

Winter (December - March) is the most popular time to visit the park because that's when the monkeys soak in the onsen, but you can visit any time of year. Baby macaques are born in the spring and are super cute to watch. By summer and fall, the babies are big enough to run and play.

For a longer stay near the Monkey Park, you can book a ryokan in the area to experience traditional Japanese hospitality.

Fun Fact: Despite generally disliking being wet, the macaques are drawn to the warm onsen during cold weather. Their thick fur helps them dry off quickly and stay warm after leaving the water.

Arashiyama Bamboo Grove

Also called Sagano Bamboo Forest, this beautiful place is located in Kyoto. There is no admission fee to walk the 400-meter (1/4-mile) path, but it does get crowded. It's best to go in the early morning and on a weekday. The path is open 24 hours a day. Sometimes at night, the pathway is lit up with lanterns. So, in order to experience the serenity shown in this photo, you have to carefully select the time you visit.

Fun Fact: The forest primarily consists of mōsō bamboo, one of the fastest-growing bamboo types. It can shoot up impressively fast, sometimes growing up to 1 meter (about 3 feet) in a single day during its peak growth season!

Cherry Blossoms

Cherry blossom season is a big deal in Japan and a favourite time for people to visit. Imagine seeing beautiful pink flowers blooming all over!

The timing of the blossoms depends a lot on the weather, so when they are at their best can vary from place to place. Usually, though, cherry blossoms show off their pretty petals for about two weeks, starting at the end of March and sometimes lasting until May.

"Hanami" is the Japanese word for "flower viewing." During this season, there are Hanami festivals all over Japan. People celebrate by walking around parks and having picnics under the cherry blossom trees. It's like a big outdoor party with nature!

Japanese Etiquette

Etiquette is an expected rule of politeness. In Japan, there are etiquette rules that you may find strange. It's good to learn them, so you are a polite guest in their country. Here are just a few pointers to help you:

Please be quiet. Being quiet is polite in Japan, even in busy places like a crowded metro train. So, always try to remember to keep your voice down.

Clean up after yourself. Never leave a mess behind. In a restaurant, look to see if there is a place where customers return their dishes. If there is, follow along and bring your dishes there when you finish eating.

Remove your shoes. Always take your shoes off when you enter someone's home. Most hosts will offer you a pair of slippers to wear inside. Ryokans and restaurants may also require you to remove your shoes when you enter. So pay attention. If there's a genkan (page 13), use it.

Line up in an orderly fashion. Lining up (queueing) is a way of life in Japan. Pay attention when you see a line, and fall in at the back (never try to cut in).

Don't walk and eat at the same time. Enjoy your food and sit somewhere to eat it. Also, don't eat or drink on local trains.

Slurping is perfectly fine in Japan. Although it may be considered rude at home, slurping shows that you are really enjoying your food. So slurp away!

Take your trash with you. Trash cans aren't common on Japanese streets or in parks. Always take your garbage with you until you can dispose of it properly.

Never blow your nose in public. It is considered very rude in Japan. If you need to blow your nose, it's best to do it in a restroom.

Tips for Travellers

Are reservations required? When you're creating your list of things to do in Japan, research whether or not reservations are required. Did you know that the Pokemon Cafe requires a reservation, and often more than a month in advance? Tokyo Disney does not sell tickets at the gate. But you can buy your tickets up to four months ahead online.

Bring an umbrella and waterproof shoes. Summertime in Japan is the rainy season. June is the rainiest month of the year. Be sure your shoes aren't mesh, or your feet will be soaked when a sudden rainstorm hits.

Carry cash for vending machines. There are vending machines everywhere in Japan. Even at the top of Mount Fuji! So be prepared and carry coins and small bills.

Carry your own bags. Japanese stores have to charge for bags, so save money and bring your own. Also, carry a few small bags to keep your trash in (doggy bags are good for this).

Pack light. Japan is often crowded, and accommodations are small. Learn to pack your things in a smaller suitcase. You'll find it much easier to get around.

Check the expiry date. Japan has some fun and unique snacks that you might want to take home as souvenirs or give to your friends back home. But in Japan, they don't use many preservatives, so be sure you check the expiration date before you buy. Better yet, buy snack souvenirs at the airport just before you go home.

Konbinis (convenience stores) have great food. It's worth trying!

Plastic food. Outside, many restaurants in Japan display plastic food. This gives you an idea of the type of food they sell. Use this to point out if you have any questions or would like to try something that looks amazing.

Public Holidays

In Japan, public holidays mean schools, government services, banks, and many businesses close down.

With 16 public holidays, it's helpful to know these dates when planning a trip:

January 1 New Year's Day Many businesses close for at least three days. Schools also shut down for winter break for about two weeks surrounding New Year.

2nd Monday in January Coming of Age Until recently, Japanese people became adults at the age of 20. But since 2022, the age has been lowered to 18. Although it's a public holiday for everyone in Japan, it's extra special for 18-year-olds!

February 11 National Foundation Day Celebrates the day it is believed Emperor Jimmu was crowned in 660 BCE (see page 19).

February 23 Emperor's Birthday The current Emperor, Naruhito was born on February 23, so this is a public holiday. This holiday will change when a new Emperor is crowned.

March 20 (approximately) Spring Equinox Day. The day the sun crosses the equator, and day and night are equal lengths.

Golden Week Combines four public holidays and is observed at the end of April and into May.

- **April 19, Showa Day** the birthday of Emperor Hirohito
- **May 3, Constitution Day**
- **May 4, Greenery Day**
- **May 5, Children's Day**

3rd Monday in July Ocean Day also called Marine Day. A day to appreciate the ocean, often spent at the beach. The day might include releasing floating lanterns.

August 11 Mountain Day A day to appreciate the mountains and nature.

3rd Monday in September Respect for the Aged Day A day to honor and appreciate the elderly.

September 23 (approximately) Autumn Equinox Day The day the sun crosses the equator once again, and day and night are equal lengths.

2nd Monday in October Health and Sports Day
Encourages people to be healthy and active.

November 3 Culture Day A day that recognizes the arts.

November 23 Labour Thanksgiving Day A day to celebrate the fall harvest and thank the country's workers.

Fun Fact: Although many Japanese celebrate Christmas, and the stores decorate for the season, Christmas and other religious holidays are not public holidays in Japan.

Manga and Anime

Manga are Japanese comic books or graphic novels, and they're usually printed in black and white, unless it's a special edition.

What's cool about manga is that they're different from the comics you might be used to. You read manga from back to front and from right to left, which is pretty unique!

Manga are sorted into categories based on who they're for. For example, Shonen manga are made for tween and teen boys, with popular ones like "Dragon Ball," "Fullmetal Alchemist," "Naruto," and "My Hero Academia."

Shojo manga is aimed at tween and teen girls, with favourites like "Sailor Moon," "Fruits Basket," "Say I Love You," and "Skip Beat."

For younger kids, there is Kodomomuke manga, and a well-known one is "Pokemon."

When a manga gets really popular, it can be turned into an anime (cartoon). "Sailor Moon" and "Dragon Ball" are famous examples of manga that became anime.

Fun fact: Pokemon first appeared as a Gameboy game in 1996. After that, it turned into a manga series, then a trading card game, and finally, an anime series.

While you can find English manga in Japan, getting the original back-to-front Japanese versions can be a fun souvenir to bring back from your trip!

Geishas

Geisha (gey-shah) means "art person." They are entertainers who perform elegant dances, play music, and engage in conversation. They mostly work in tea houses.

Geishas have been part of Japanese culture for hundreds of years. You can spot them because they wear beautiful silk kimonos and white makeup. The reason for the white makeup is that before there was electricity, long ago, it would show off their faces better under candlelight.

It takes years of training for a woman to become a geisha, and there are also strict rules. For example, a geisha has to be single. So, if they marry one day, they would have to quit their geisha job.

Kimonos

Kimonos (kee-mo-nos) are traditional robes that are important to Japanese culture. Made from silk, cotton, or other fabrics, they have designs with symbols with special meanings based on the occasion.

While not worn daily, kimonos are often worn for special events like weddings. Their design has been the same for hundreds of years and includes long flowing sleeves and a waist sash called an 'obi.'

Putting on a kimono isn't simple; it's an art that some learn in special schools. People often need help dressing in a formal kimono to make sure it's worn correctly.

Accessories are also important when wearing a kimono. Traditional shoes and, for women, hair ornaments like 'kanzashi' complete the look.

Japanese Myths and Legends

Japan has a deep tradition of stories, myths and legends. It would take an entire book to re-tell some of them. One of the most famous myths tells about how the Earth was created. So here is a very chopped-down summary of how the Earth began, according to Japanese mythology:

It all started with a couple of Gods named Izanagi and Izanami. They used a spear to stir the ocean, which created land masses.

The couple later fell in love and had children. But Izanami died when she gave birth to the God of Fire. Izanagi was very sad when she died, and he began to cry. Three new Gods were born from his tears: Amaterasu, the Sun Goddess; Tsukuyomi, the Moon God; and Susanoo, the God of Seas and Storms. They were called the Three Noble Children.

But like all brothers and sisters, they would fight. One day, Amaterasu (sun) and Tsukuyomi (moon) had such a big fight that they decided not to talk to each other anymore. So they each moved to different sides of the Earth. This is why the sun and the moon are never together, and we have days and nights.

Again, like all brothers and sisters, there was jealousy. Susanoo was jealous because everyone loved Amaterasu, so he stormed to her house to fight. Susanoo lost the fight, so he became furious. He destroyed everything his sister had, including her weaving hall, which killed one of the weavers.

Amaterasu was so sad that she left her home and took herself to a cave, plunging the world into darkness. After she had been gone for some time, the Earth experienced its first winter because Amaterasu wasn't around to make everything warm and bright.

All the other Gods had to figure out how to get Amaterasu out of the cave. So they had a big party, laughed, and danced outside the cave. Curiosity finally got to Amaterasu, so she peeked out of the cave to see what was happening. That's when she saw the most beautiful Goddess she'd ever seen, shining brightly and making everyone happy. She realized it was a mirror when she walked closer to the Goddess. That's when she knew how important she was and decided to stay out of the cave.

Now that they had their sun Goddess back, it was time for the Gods to deal with Susanoo. They punished him and threw him out.

Meanwhile, Susanoo met a beautiful woman named Kushinada-hime and wanted to marry her. But Yamata-no-Orochi, an eight-headed dragon, was coming to eat her, so Susanoo had to kill the dragon. He was successful and saved Kushinada-hime's life. While he cut off the dragon's tail, he found a magic sword. The sword, Kusanagi-no-Tsurugi, became the Imperial Regalia* of Japan.

Wanting to make things right with his sister, Susanoo gave Amaterasu the sword as an apology. Now everyone was happy. Amaterasu led a good life and had more children. One of her descendants was Jimmu, who became the first Emperor of Japan.

* Regalia is a symbol of royalty, like a crown for example.

Origami

Origami is the art of paper folding. It's not certain if it originated in Japan, but it has been an important part of Japanese culture for hundreds of years. Originally, the paper was expensive, so origami was only used for religious ceremonies. But today, it is a fun pastime all over the world.

If you want to learn more about origami, you can get books and videos. You can also do an online search and see if you can find instructions for a project that interests you.

Origami requires patience. In the next few pages, we've provided instructions for one origami project. Give it a try!

How to Make an Origami Heart

Would you like to try some origami? Here's a project for you: It's a paper heart!

We'll start with a square piece of paper. To make it easier, try to find a piece of paper that is coloured on one side and white on the other. If you only have white paper, try to colour or draw on one side with markers, and leave the other side blank.

Step 1: With the colour side down, fold the right side of the paper over to the left. Run your finger along the folded edge to make a crease. Then, unfold it so you have a square again.

Step 2: Now fold the bottom edge up to the top edge. Make another crease, and unfold it so you have a square again.

Step 3: With the colour side down, bring the bottom up to the crease in the centre of the paper.

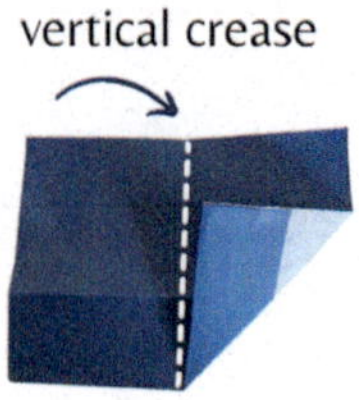

Step 4: Flip the paper over so the colour side faces up. Now, fold the bottom right corner up to meet the vertical crease.

Step 5: Do the same on the left side. Remember to make a crease with each fold.

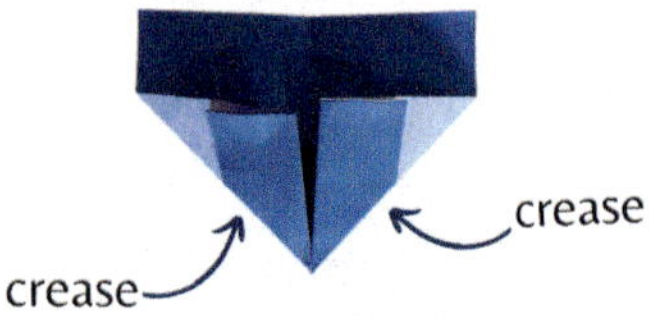

Step 6: Flip the paper over so it looks like this.

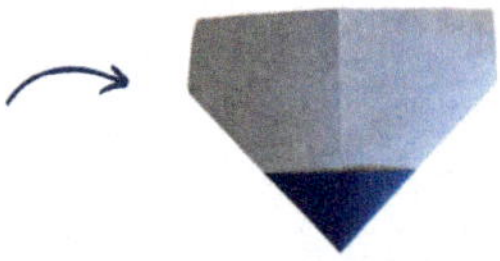

Step 7: Fold the left and right edges so they meet in the middle. Make a crease on each side.

Step 8: Fold the top left and right corners inward and make creases.

Step 9: Bring the top point down to the bottom point and start to flatten it down.

Step 10: Lift the top point and insert it into the lower pocket.

This is what your heart should look like by now.

Step 11: Flatten the top section of the heart.

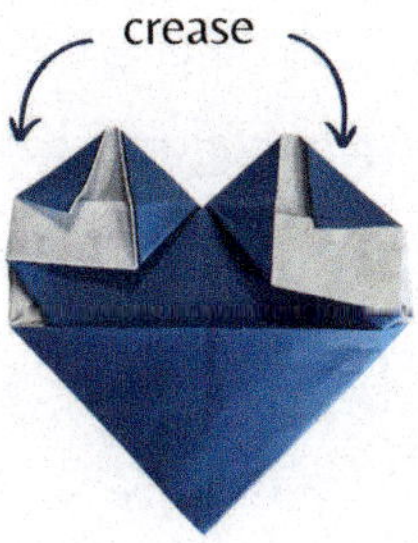

Step 12: Fold the top left and right corners inward and make creases.

Step 13: Fold the two top points of the heart down a little and make creases.

Flip it over, and there you have it: An origami heart!

Famous Japanese Inventions

The Japanese people have made so many contributions to modern society worldwide. Here are just a few inventions, some we use every day, that we can thank Japan for:

Masahiro Hara invented the **QR Code** (quick response code) in 1994. He was working at a company that helped make cars and needed a faster way to keep track of car parts. One day, while playing a game called Go, he got an idea...

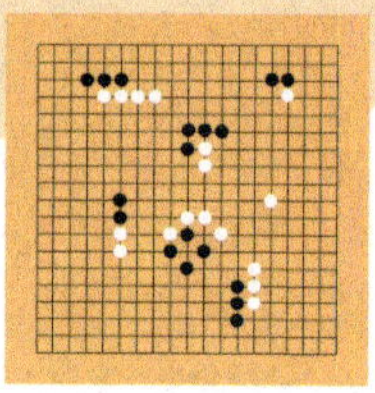

Emojis were invented by Shigetaka Kurita in 1999. Shigetaka worked for a phone company and created the first set of emojis for their mobile phones and pagers.

Fun Fact: The word emoji combines two Japanese words: "picture" and "letter". It's just a coincidence that the word is similar to "emotion" in English.

Karaoke (kah-rah-oh-keh) was invented by Daisuke Inoue in the early 1970s. He was a musician who came up with the idea of a machine that lets people sing along to music without live bands. This invention quickly became a fun activity enjoyed all over the world!

Hideo Shima played a big part in creating the Shinkansen, also known as the **Bullet Train**, which started running in 1964. People needed a fast way to travel for the Tokyo Olympics, and that's when the super-speedy Bullet Train came in handy!

Fun Fact: Japanese Bullet Trains are not only super fast but are also among the safest trains in the world.

Toshiba invented the **electric rice cooker** in 1955. Before this, cooking rice required a lot of time and care, especially since rice is a staple food in Japan, and instant rice wasn't a thing. With the new rice cooker, people no longer had to spend hours in the kitchen, making rice cooking much easier and faster. Now, almost every kitchen in Japan has a rice cooker.

Robots: Japan is a leader in robotics. One famous robot is ASIMO, developed by Honda. He can walk, run, and perform tasks with human-like movements.

The first **Capsule Hotel** was designed by Kisho Kurokawa and opened in 1979. These hotels were created to solve the problem of limited space and affordability.The first capsule hotel was in Osaka, Japan, but now they can be found all over the world.

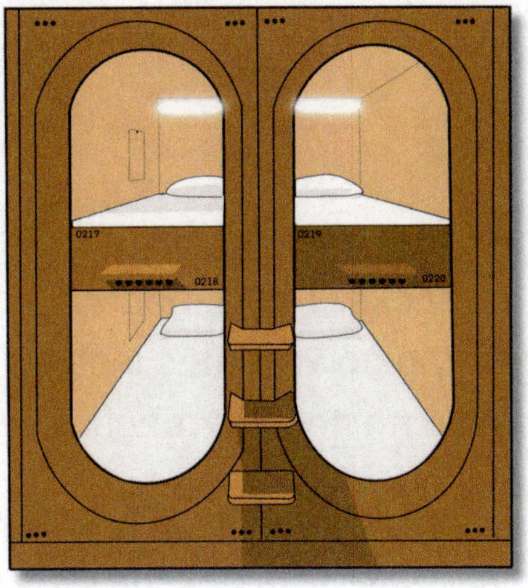

Tactile Paving was invented in 1965 by Seiichi Miyake. It's used at train stations, near stairs, and any other public place a blind person needs to be aware of.

Although they have been used in Japan since the 60's, it took Western countries like Canada and the U.S. until the 1990s before they became common.

Japanese Chopsticks

Shape

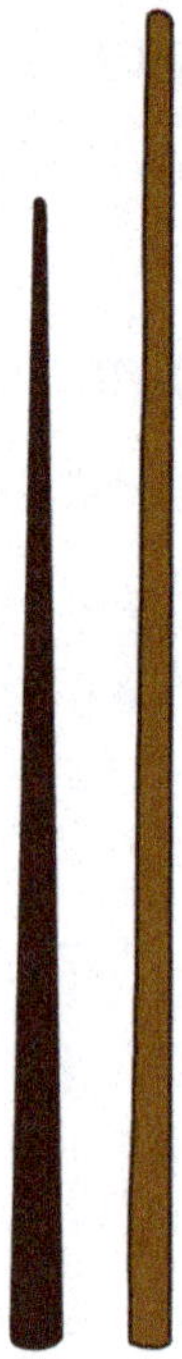

Japanese chopsticks are shorter than Chinese chopsticks. This is because, in Japan, people eat from their own plates instead of sharing a plate. So there's no need to reach very far.

Japanese chopsticks are also more pointy at the ends compared to Chinese chopsticks. The reason is that many Japanese meals have small, whole fish. The pointy sticks make it easier to pick out the bones.

Chopstick Etiquette (rules of politeness)

Never rest your chopsticks across your bowl or leave them sticking in your food. Instead, use a chopstick rest or lay the tips on the left side of your plate.

Never put chopsticks in your mouth. It is considered rude to lick food off your chopsticks.

Learn to use chopsticks properly. Never stab your food.

Don't point your chopsticks at anyone. When you lay them on the table, put them down horizontally, not vertically.

How to Use Chopsticks

There are many different ways to hold chopsticks. Here we show you the "standard grip."

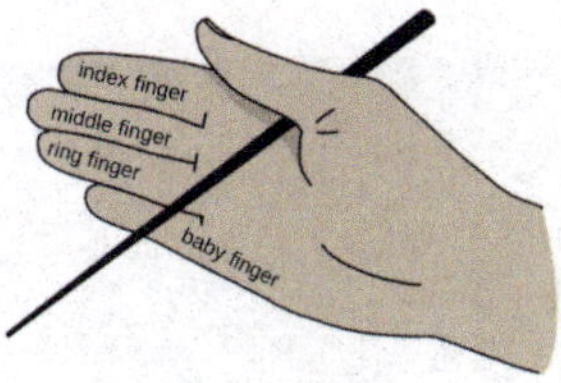

Step 1: Put one chopstick under your thumb and let it rest on your palm.

Step 2: Bend your baby finger and ring finger under the first chopstick to give it support.

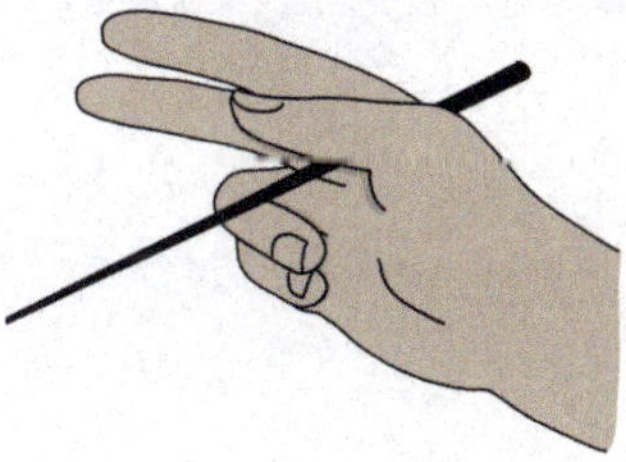

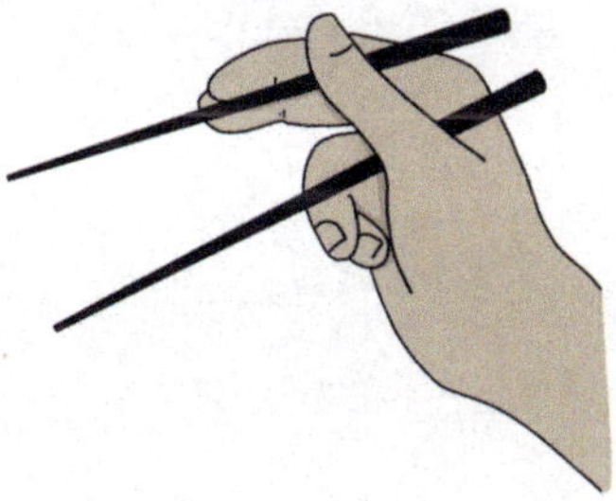

Step 3: Place the second chopstick on top, between your thumb and index and middle finger.

Step 4: Move your middle finger down so it supports the bottom of the chopstick.

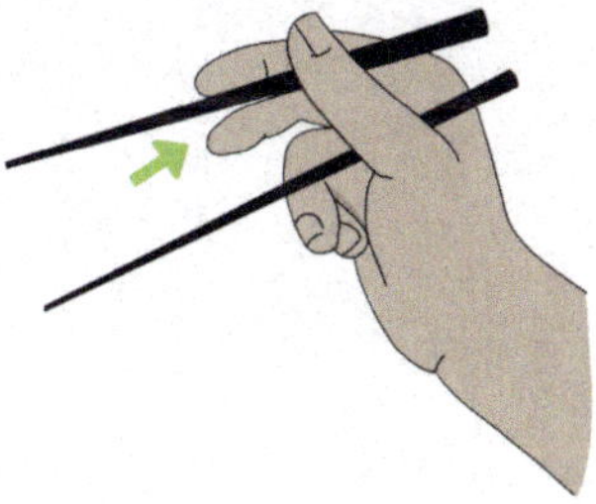

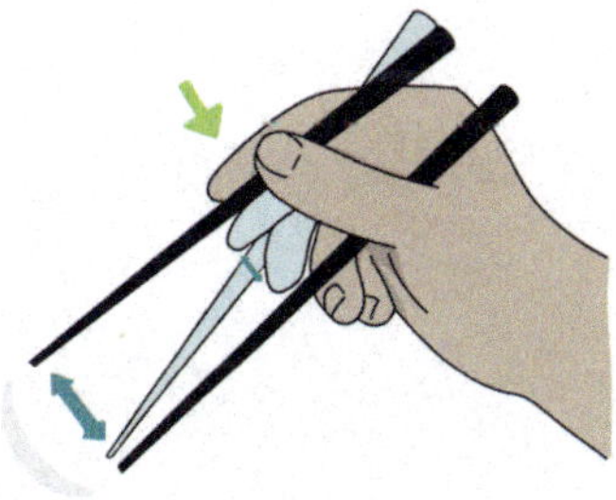

Step 5: Move your index finger up and down to meet the tip of the lower chopstick.

Japanese Food

Now that we know how to use chopsticks let's explore some of the most popular food in Japan. Here are some common things you'll find in a Japanese restaurant:

RICE

- SUSHI (MADE WITH FISH OR VEGETABLES)
- DONBURI (RICE BOWL WITH FISH, MEAT OR VEGETABLES)
- ONIGIRI (RICE BALLS OFTEN WRAPPED IN SEAWEED)
- CHAZUKE (GREEN TEA OR WATER POURED OVER RICE)

SEAFOOD

- SASHIMI (RAW, OFTEN INCLUDES SALMON, TUNA, HALIBUT OR SQUID)
- YAKIZAKANA (GRILLED FISH)
- UNAGI (GRILLED EEL)

NOODLES

- SOBA (BUCKWHEAT CAN BE SERVED HOT OR COLD))
- UDON (THICK AND CHEWY MADE WITH WHEAT)
- RAMEN (SERVED IN BROTH OFTEN WITH SLICED PORK)
- SOMEN (VERY THIN, SERVED COLD)

YAKINIKU (GRILLED MEAT)

- YAKITORI (CHICKEN)
- TONKATSU (BREADED, DEEP-FRIED PORK)
- NIKUJAGA (STEWED DISH, MADE WITH BEEF & POTATOES)

TOFU

- MISO SOUP (OFTEN INCLUDES SEAWEED & GREEN ONIONS)
- HIYAYAKKO (COLD TOFU TOPPED WITH GRATED GINGER)
- YUDOFU (TOFU SIMMERED IN BROTH & SERVED WITH DIPPING SAUCES)

Sushi

Chazuke

Salmon Sashimi

Ramen

Tonkatsu

Miso Soup

Sayonara! Goodbye!

We hope you enjoyed your exploration of Japan. Considered one of the top ten safest countries in the world*, Japan is ideal for families who travel with kids. If you're going to Japan, you will have the experience of a lifetime!

*According to the Global Peace Index (GPI), 2023.

About the Author

Collette is a world traveller and a proud G-Mom to Julien and Beau! She loves to write about travelling and is excited to help inspire others to embrace their inner explorer. Having visited all seven continents, she now enjoys travel through the eyes of her grandsons. They inspire and like to share their thoughts and opinions on what should be included in each Learn About the World Series book.

To see more books in this series, scan the QR code below.

Please leave an honest review on Amazon; it will go a long way to creating more books like this one.

Acknowledgements:

Pg 5 "500 yen bicolor clad coin obverse" by Heavy Frisker is licensed under CC BY-SA 4.0.
Pg 12 "Japanese traditional style house interior design / 和風建築(わふうけんちく)" by TANAKA Juuyoh (田中十洋) is licensed under CC BY 2.0.
Pg 13 "Japanese traditional style SAMURAI house / 稲葉家下屋敷(いなばけ しもやしき)" by TANAKA Juuyoh (田中十洋) is licensed under CC BY 2.0.
Pg. 13 "butsudan" by nash1011 is licensed under CC BY 2.0.
Pg. 13 "Home - 玄関 - Genkan (Entrée)" by chacrebleu is licensed under CC BY-SA 2.0.
Pg. 14 "Japanese toilet" by tdhedengren is licensed under CC BY-SA 2.0.
Pg. 14 "Japanese-Style: Standard Room Bathroom" by nishimuraya.kinosakionsen is licensed under CC BY 2.0.
Pg 23 "Japanese Alps" by 雷太 is licensed under CC BY 2.0.
Pg 23 "Japan's Beautiful Coastline" by kvn.jns is licensed under CC BY 2.0.
Pg 23 "2021 Sagano Bamboo forest in Arashiyama, Kyoto, Japan" by Naokijp is licensed under CC BY-SA 4.0.
Pg 24 "File:Fishing on Lake Biwa - DSC06972.JPG" by Daderot is marked with CC0 1.0.
Pg 24 "Shinagawa City – Japan" by williamcho is licensed under CC BY-SA 2.0.
Pg 24 "Terraced Rice Fields in Ishibu" by izunavi is licensed under CC BY 2.0.
Pg 37 "snow monkeys hot tubbing" by edskoch is licensed under CC BY 2.0.
Pg 46 "One Piece collection in manga shop" by DocChewbacca is licensed under CC BY-SA 2.0.

LEARN ABOUT JAPAN

For Kids

ISBN 978-1-7390565-6-8

Printed in Great Britain
by Amazon

49364396R00044